31 Days of Surrender
Respecting Life Every Day

by

Michael B. Allen

POSITIVE PUSH PRESS

Positive Push Press LLC
©2024 by Michael B. Allen
Publisher Cataloging-in-Publication Data
Name: Allen, Michael, B., author
Title: 31 Days of Surrender: Respecting Life Every Day
Description: First edition | Atlanta, GA: Positive Push Press, LLC, 2024 | Includes Index.
Print (paperback) ISBN 978-0-9798358-1-0
eBook ISBN 978-0-9798358-4-1

Positive Push Press, LLC.
P. O. Box 422054
Atlanta, Georgia 30342
U.S.A.

www.positivepushpress.com
info@positivepushpress.com

The author does not endorse or recommend any products, processes, or services. Therefore, any mention of products, processes, or services in this book should not be construed as an endorsement or recommendation. The author provides links to websites for informational purposes only. Although every reasonable effort is made to present current and accurate information, the author makes no guarantees of any kind and cannot be held liable for any outdated or incorrect information. This publication is intended to provide guidance as it relates to the topics being presented. It is sold with the understanding that the author and publisher are not herein engaged in rendering legal or psychological advice. The author and publisher disclaim any personal liability, directly or indirectly, for advice or information presented within.

Cover design by Osadolor Iyahen
Book / eBook formatting by Henrietta Sampson

This book is dedicated to my mother Hazel D. Rimes, my dad Ernest Lee Allen, my sisters Deborah and Marveen, and of course to my son Zachary. Each of you have been the greatest inspirations in my life! I am also dedicating this book to parents, children, and educators everywhere.

Table of Contents

Foreword

By Derrick C. Manning

I often wonder how people as individuals, groups, organizations, neighborhoods, communities, states, countries, and even continents, as far as that matters, can embrace a spirit of evilness. The hate, biases, bullying, envy, vindictiveness, and sense of superiority needed to think that one ethnicity is better than another simply amazes my soul. I, for one, have to reflect on how I have been able to develop a deep thirst for peace, harmony, joy, love, personal improvement, and ultimately, wanting for others what I want for myself. I am genuinely excited to see others thrive in every aspect of life and persistently seek means to help those who are less fortunate.

Naturally, I attribute my love for others to my parents, my siblings, and of course, my paternal journey with my children; however, there is one cousin in particular who my family and I have esteemed to be a model for peace, joy, and salvation: Michael B. Allen.

Michael and I have been like brothers for as long as I can remember. We are brothers by the blood of Jesus in our Christian faith, as alumni of Florida Agricultural and Mechanical University, and through the Phi Beta Sigma fraternity. Michael B. Allen is my first cousin and has always been one of my most loyal and greatest inspirations. I don't recall a time in my life when Michael wasn't present and wasn't the epitome of compassion for others.

I believe it is by the glory of the Holy Spirit that Michael felt a calling from God to share his conviction for peace, joy, and salvation, not only for the nurturing of his spirit but for the love of all people in general. This heartfelt book, *31 Days of Surrender: Respecting Life Every Day*, came into vision during one of our typical conversations of uplifting and supporting one another through perhaps some of the most challenging times of our lives. Thus, it is my fervent belief that this giftedly crafted and soulful creation will fill your soul with thoughts of kindness, preservation of all life, and vehement rejection of hate to any degree.

Michael coined the expression "Surrender Your Hate" and embraced this concept as a purpose placed on his life. In my estimation, the reflections illustrated in *31 Days of Surrender: Respecting Life Every Day* are prefaced by a pledge for all to openly acknowledge a belief in the power of love. More abundantly, the book clearly outlines a platform for parents, our first teachers and role models, to impact the lives of their children by guiding conscious thought as it connects with the management of our emotions. Perhaps the pure essence of our beliefs, values, morals we practice, and how we interact with others is predicated on when, how, where, and who we allow to pour into our consciousness. We are who we are because of the seeds sown by our parents and the learned behavior modeled by those we love the most. My parents often referenced a Bible verse that became a favorite of mine, Proverbs 22:6: "Train up a child in the way he should go: and when he is old, he will not depart from it." Unfortunately, this phenomenon is as common among those with evil mindsets as it is among those that embrace the concept of surrendering hate by virtue of the

31 reflections outlined in this amazing book. I believe this is why Michael B. Allen feels a deep sense of conviction to share his vision of harmony and love with all mankind.

Lastly, I am earnestly grateful to be granted the opportunity to provide the foreword to *31 Days of Surrender: Respecting Life Every Day*. I implore each of you to join Michael B. Allen, myself, and society as a whole as we pledge our commitment to refuting hate and respecting life every day.

Introduction

This book, *31 Days of Surrender*, is for two sets of people: parents and children. I believe this group of people – grandparents, parents, and the children we produce – are generationally affected by the ongoing, continual, senseless deaths and killings of our family members. Violence, of all types, that comes from uncontrolled anger, hate, hateful actions, prejudices, biases, and what was once a simple dislike for another person (regardless of the reason or reasons) has led many people to choose gun violence (murder) to solve our disagreements and conflicts.

All of this produces unnecessary trauma. We must learn to manage our anger when we perceive we are in a conflict with another human being. Please see the other person as just that: another human being, created by God. Just like the actor in a shooting, who commits the life-ending violence that comes from the use of a gun to resolve whatever angry conflict or situation they may find themselves in with another person.

The perpetrator of a shooting needs our help to learn the value of life, both theirs and that of the person or people they are planning to kill. I pray this book helps someone make the right decision *not* to commit a life-ending, life-changing act of violence toward another human being.

You may ask, as I'm sure some people will, why write this book or share this message in this manner? This question can be answered by the death of George Floyd in Minneapolis, Minnesota on May 25, 2020. As the knee and full body weight of a Minneapolis police officer pressed on the neck of Mr. Floyd, taking away his life's breath, I knew then that I could no longer remain silent. As a parent myself and as a child of my parents, I had to take as positive of action as I could to help change this kind of open hatred that takes the life of someone else's parent or child.

As the killing of Mr. Floyd was happening, God spoke to me and said that he represents all of humanity in this instance – parent or child, parent and child. He instructed me to go and tell the world to surrender its hate to preserve and continue the lives of all humanity. God directed me to surrender my hate and anger and to tell the world (or as many of the eight billion souls on Earth as possible) to surrender. Let go, give up the hateful feelings, emotions, and actions that cause the killing of His created humanity, young, old, male, female, parent, or child, for the rest of our earthly existence.

WOW! Wow is right. I said the same thing to God when He commanded me to share this message with the world. I asked him if he was telling me to surrender my hate, dislike, bias, and prejudice. He said, yes, I am, but I'm also telling you to take this message of love over hate, this idea of how people are to live in harmony, peace, and love without killing each other to all who will listen, hear, and respond in His obedience to "letting life live."

I also asked Him, how am I to do this, and He has begun to answer this question with the following direction and actions:

1. Start a business and call it Surrender Your Hate.
2. Develop a website (www.surrenderyourhate.com) and offer message merchandise to spread love. Use the website to reach people and share strategies and techniques to manage anger and conflict.
3. Share the message on social media.
4. Write a book or books on the subject.
5. Conduct trainings on conflict management, de-escalation strategies, and relationship building.
6. Work with and partner with TV, radio, business leaders, government officials, celebrities, influencers, sports figures, musicians, churches, pastors, priests, places of worship and other mission-oriented organizations, groups, and individuals.
7. Start Let Life Live, Inc. as a nonprofit to further the message of Surrender Your Hate and that life is God's gift of infinite value!

I have begun each of these actions. I will need each of you to become warriors, ambassadors, witnesses, and peacemakers for God's message to humanity: stop killing each other, love others as He loves us, do unto others as you would have others do to you!

God and I want each of us to live our daily lives focused on Him, not on the issues of life that anger us nor the hatred we carry in our hearts and spirits. God wants us to live in peace and love, for love conquers hate and love will have its eternal victory at the end of our earthly lives. Love wins!

This is why I wrote this book. This is the message of loving actions He and I want us to take as we interact with each other all around the world.

I hope you find this message inspiring. I pray the message contained in this book and in the vision, mission, and purpose of Surrender Your

Hate will further answer the questions of what, why, and how for you. I hope that these three words (Surrender Your Hate) stir up in your spirit and cause you to act and to teach others to be respecters and protectors of life, to *Surrender Your Hate* and model behaviors of peace and love which may help another person see value in another life, and in their own life.

Now, if you are so moved, please join the Surrender Your Hate movement! You can begin by taking the Surrender Your Hate Pledge and by reading and sharing this book with a parent or a child you know. Each one, teach one the basics of human civility: respect for life and humanity, showing kindness, and expressing peace and love every day.

Do these things daily and you will help yourself and others experience the life-saving power of *31 Days of Surrender*!

While I don't know your specific situation, my hope is that by reading this book you will be able to come up with solutions and ideas that work for you and your family. The first part of the book covers 31 daily reflections. The second part of the book delves deeper into what is required to respect life every day. In this section, you will explore how to make the right decisions, manage anger, think beyond what you see, examine de-escalation techniques, recognize what it means to let life live, and review what hate is and how to stand against it. Lastly, you will be presented with ideas on how to resolve conflict peacefully.

Earlier in the introduction to *31 Days of Surrender*, I spoke to those of us who are parents or grandparents and each of us as children. Make no mistake in understanding who this book is intended to inspire to action. I believe each of us as a member of the human race (all eight billion souls) can benefit from the reflections, short stories, and actionable steps included here. The desire is to have each of us begin to assist in the reduction, and hopeful prevention of gun violence. Those of you who are children but not parents, this book is for you too! Simply because you carry the title of child. Your involvement may be as a guardian, mentor, neighbor, friend, or concerned human being. Take action! Read this book. Share this book. Get involved. Model the way to peace through your behaviors of surrendering hate, showing love, and respecting life.

Surrender Your Hate Pledge

I pledge to surrender my hate in any and every form. I make this pledge to God and humanity. I will let life live, regardless of differences, and I will choose to live in peace every day with my fellow human. I believe love conquers all hate.

Part One

31 DAYS OF
SURRENDER

31 Days of Surrender

Thirty-one reflections follow. Focus on these with your children. You don't necessarily need to go in order, day by day. You can spend time with one topic on more than one day or reflect on several topics in a day. The idea is that you work through all the topics with your children. Meditate and look within as you review the day's focus area, and engage in conversations with your family and yourself.

Reflection doesn't always mean writing down your ideas. This is why you will not see a space to write in every day. This is your personal journey, so interact with the text in a manner that best fits you and your children. Some days you may spend time quietly reflecting on the topic, while other days you may talk about the topics while driving. Additionally, you may talk with your kids about something and choose to write down your thoughts. Alternatively, you may spend time with God and be led to worship and pray. It is totally up to you. The most important thing is that you read, reflect, and create your own meaning for you and your children.

Please note that your children may not mean your biological children. It might not even mean children that live with you. Your children may be the kids in your neighborhood, community, church, or other family members' children. It might be the kid that passes in front of your house on his or her way to school. Even if you don't have kids of your own, you still have the opportunity to make a positive difference in their lives.

Learn how to grow closer to God and help make the world a better place for all. I believe every day is a day of surrender! I encourage prayer, praise, and worship (devotion) throughout each day to grow closer to God, Jesus, and the Holy Spirit. This relationship helps you control your emotions, feelings, and thoughts. This daily act of surrender will help each of us make this world a more peaceful place to *Let Life Live*! Join me on this daily journey of surrender. *Peace and love to and for all of God's creation!*

Day 1

Faith

*"Now faith is the substance of things hoped
for, the evidence of things not seen."*

(HEBREWS 11:1 KJV)

What is faith to you? How does your faith direct you on a daily basis? My faith directs me all throughout each day. I am conscious of my relationship with God. I want to please God by living in peace and love with all humans, every day. This desire helps shape my behavior when I'm interacting with others.

Do you remember the campaign that asked the question "what would Jesus do?" WWJD? Google it if you are unfamiliar. As for me, I'm old enough to remember this insightful question. This question makes me respond by living my life based on His principles, His commandment to love and not hate.

Have faith. Believe in the good. This act of good intent toward another will slowly end the desire to harm another. Yes, again, I know, easier said than done – but give it a try anyway. We will all be better for making an attempt to let life live and surrendering our hate (prejudice, bias, dislike, etc.) every day!

The greatest test of my faith came when my oldest sister Deborah was passing away. My mother appointed me the decision maker as to when or if to remove her from life support. I didn't want this assignment, but because of my obedience to my mom and the fact that I had some experience as a pharmaceutical/medical professional, I accepted the most difficult directive of my life. After much prayer and supplication to God, I was led to make the ultimate and final decision. Without my faith in God and my belief that my sister was heaven bound, I would not have been able to make this life-ending decision. I was able to give the order to remove her life support, thus ending her earthly life because of my faith.

I thought this was the most difficult time of my life, two weeks later my dad died! A double whammy of grief and tests of my faith. Death tries us; our faith, beliefs, strength, courage, resolve, and many more emotions. Yet still, we must have faith that God's plan is greater than our plan. These faith challenges took place in 2009.

My most recent tests of faith came when my mother was dying from dementia/Alzheimer's. To make this situation even more complex and challenging, I almost passed away before her due to Covid! 2021 is now the greatest test of my faith in my 60 years of life. My sister's passing, my dad's passing, and then my momma. God tests us – daily! This is why we all must have faith in Him more so than we do ourselves or others.

We as loving, caring humans all mean well, but end of life experiences can really test our faith and our belief in everything, including God.

I encourage you, friend, have faith no matter what, because His plan for your life is far greater than yours!

Have you had a life-changing faith test yet? How did you or will you handle it? I am encouraging you to turn to God and surrender your life and understanding to Him. Praying constantly and listening to Godly counsel will help you through your faith test(s). *Have faith!* Having faith has strengthened and encouraged me to keep moving forward – every day I surrender to His will for my life.

Have faith that God will fight your battles. You don't have to seek revenge or take matters into your own hands. It takes faith to remain calm in the midst of being mistreated, disrespected, or wronged. As parents, one of the most important lessons we can teach our children is the lesson of faith. You should seek to be a continual example of faith in action. Today's world is filled with violence, rage, and anger. You can watch the news and see sad examples of people taking revenge and getting even, ultimately leading to death. The world would be a better place if we learned to live by faith and walked in peace and love.

Ask your kids: what does faith mean to them? Share an example of faith with them from your perspective.

Record your reflections here.

Day 2

Compassion

Offer it, give it, be it – compassionate.

What does compassion mean to you? While you ponder your answer to this question, allow me to offer my understanding of this powerful word. Compassion suggests the shared understanding or feeling of the suffering and challenges of another person. Feeling and caring for what another is going through as they go through life. It is an internal emotion of caring about someone else's pain in a deep, heartfelt sense. Each human, I believe, has an inborn measure of compassion that needs to be expressed daily. We all must be more willing to show someone that we care about them truthfully.

Ask yourself, as I asked earlier, what does compassion mean to you? Answer this question in your own words. Then think about how you can show compassion to someone: family member, friend, co-worker, or stranger. Now go about your day with this idea of expressing kindness and your definition of compassion. Remember, everyone has a story they are living and, at some point, needs to know that someone cares about what they are going through.

You need compassion and so does that person you see or are thinking about. Be kind today! Help someone today in dealing with what they are experiencing.

Day 3

Empathy

Understanding others from their
viewpoint and not just our own.

Empathy is very similar and related to compassion. I believe it is difficult to separate the two emotions. I don't try to make them separate or different ideas. The two words go together; one without the other can come across as disingenuous or fake. Being empathetic can make you feel sadness or pain for another person. Don't hold on to the negative emotion you feel for someone's pain because doing so can drag you down.

This is why compassion and empathy are joined together. After expressing empathy for someone, the next step or emotional response is to take a positive action to help them resolve their pain, challenge, or suffering. Don't let another's pain become your problem. Use your "feeling sorry for" (empathetic) emotion as an opportunity to listen to the person and then help them come up with a solution for what might be a sorrowful or painful situation.

Talk to your children about a time when you were empathetic to someone. Ask them to share with you how they may have showed empathy
in the past. Help them to create a true understanding of what it means
to be empathetic.

I believe empathy and compassion are intertwined. What do you think?
What do your children think? Record your thoughts here.

Day 4

Sympathy

Shared feelings for those experiencing
hardship and difficulties.

Sympathy is similar to compassion and empathy. Sympathy helps one build trust and a rapport with another person who is going through a negative experience.

Sharing your feeling of pity or sorrow with a person who is in the midst of a difficult situation gives that person a safe place to express his or her emotions and concerns. Sympathy, listening, caring, having compassion and empathy touches the heart of another. This word brings to mind the proverbial phrase "that warms my heart." It makes a person feel valued, heard, and cared for.

Sympathy, compassion, and empathy make a person who's going through difficulties feel loved. Sympathy makes the person feel a bit more comfortable with their discomfort because they start to see a picture of themselves where that difficult situation doesn't hurt as bad. Sympathy, compassion, and empathy are like three warm blankets on a very cold and dark day.

The sun is going to shine again. This too shall pass. Let someone know that a brighter day is ahead.

Day 5

Trust

*Truth, honesty, promise, confidence, belief; having
the confidence to not hurt, harm, or violate anyone.*

When I think of the concept of trust, I think of a promise kept. In the Bible, God makes many promises to man and He keeps them all! He does what He says He will do. As a child, it was instilled in me that my word must be true – my word is my bond!

As a father, when I promise my son something (anything), he knows it's going to be done. Period. Without fail! He then learns to trust and believe in what I say and do. This is my testament, my word. My bond – a spoken agreement to do what I say I'm going to do. Doing what one says builds confidence and belief. This is what inspires trust between people, between nations. An unwavering honesty in doing what is said fosters trust.

Be honest. Be truthful. Make and keep your promise or don't promise! These actions will cause others to have confidence and belief in you. When someone possesses each of the values and actions described here, it creates trust and builds a trusting relationship.

Trust God – our original promise maker and keeper!

Day 6

Respect

Respect helps us make it home
safely when conflict arises.

What exactly does it look like for another person to show, give, or offer respect? You can't see, taste, or hear respect. Or can you? I can hear it in a person's tone of voice (see tone of voice later in this book). I can see respect in a person's body language, or lack thereof, when they are threatening me. I know how I feel when I am disrespected. What is respect? For me, respect or the lack thereof affects my sense of personhood, my sense of personal value and worth. This is why this concept can be very sensitive and personal, making it difficult to know exactly when someone feels disrespected. What are we to do to show and give respect? One answer to this question is another biblical or old school answer: "Do unto others as you would have others do unto you," as stated in Luke 6:31. This sentiment and behavior is a tried-and-true method for peaceful and life-continuing interactions with another person. Give a person the regard their individuality and humanity demands, and our outcomes will be much improved!

How does one know if they are being respectful toward another? Again, the adage of do unto others helps answer this challenge. The natural anatomical apparatuses of our eyes and ears will help us see and hear whether or not we are giving or receiving respect. Finally, if your internal meter goes off and you begin to feel or think you are not giving or getting respect, then change your course by giving it or asking to receive it. I pray these ideas work for you and your societal interactions. Let's accept others so they may do the same to us!

Ask your children to describe a time when they felt disrespected, maybe at school or in the community. Help your child put into his/her own words what it means to give respect to another.

Day 7

Positivity

*Looking for solutions and expecting good results
and success. Let's look ahead to the good – daily!*

Being positive is much more than the opposite of being negative. There is a warm, radiant energy that comes forth from one's inner being when he/she has an energy that inspires the goodness, happiness, and encouragement of another's soul and spirit.

We need positive people in our lives and in our communities to affect the good. Positivity is giving and receiving goodwill – a shared goodness and happiness for all.

Day 8

Strategy

*Strategy includes spending time planning to be
kind, succeed in conflict, and produce a win-win.*

Strategy incorporates practices that will address the problem or opportunity and propose an action plan for the desired outcome. A strategy is a simple plan. It is something you can develop with your children now.

When my son was a boy, I would tell him to "think it through." What I was encouraging him to do was to see the positive outcome he wanted at the end of his challenge, issue, or problem. I encouraged him to see his challenges resolved in the manner he desired. This required him to slow down from his first thought, fear, or concern and then develop a plan as to how he would affect the ending. I wanted him to visualize the outcome he desired.

This strategic thinking and having forethought to plan a favorable outcome also helps us return home safely! If only we all could model this positive approach on a daily basis. This strategic thinking will help to reduce gun violence, hatred, bias, prejudice, and discord amongst us humans. "Think it through."

Take a while to develop high-level strategies with your children. Talk through a few situations that may require a level head and a calm mind.

Here are a few examples to get you started. You can certainly speak to your children and ask them about real-life difficulties they face each day.

Thinking It Through

WHAT WOULD YOU DO IF...   HOW SHOULD YOU RESPOND?

A CLASSMATE CALLED YOU UGLY NAMES	

SOMEONE STARTS TO HIT YOU OR PUSH YOU FOR NO REASON	

SOMEONE STEALS YOUR LAPTOP OR PHONE	

YOU READ NEGATIVE COMMENTS POSTED ABOUT YOU ON SOCIAL MEDIA	

Thinking It Through

WHAT WOULD YOU DO IF...	HOW SHOULD YOU RESPOND?
SOMEONE ASKS YOU TO CHEAT ON A TEST	
SOMEONE ASKS YOU TO TRY USING DRUGS OR DRINK ALCOHOL	
SOMEONE ASKS TO COPY YOUR WORK	
YOU KNOW SOMEONE HAS A WEAPON AT SCHOOL IN HIS/HER BOOKBAG	

35

Day 9

Hope

Is God's strategy, not man's.

Look beyond your present circumstances even when you cannot see the positive outcome you desire. Hope is another Godly principle that says, "this too shall pass", as reflected in 2 Corinthians 4:17-18. Having a sense of a positive expectation leads one to follow a righteous path to achieve it. It propels one to live with the right image and vision one sees in his/her spirit mind when faced daily with a trial, test, temptation, or challenge.

Hope overpowers hopelessness. Hope is eternal. Hopelessness is temporary and fleeting. Have you experienced hopelessness? I have. I've had many fleeting moments of hopelessness.

Whether my situation was caused by a broken heart, a divorce, a job loss, or the death of a family member or a friend, hopelessness has snuck its way into my day, my nights, my life. I've lost loves, been rejected, let go from my job, filed bankruptcy, and experienced the failure of my boyhood dream of owning my own men's clothing store.

Each of those events left me with a feeling of hopelessness. But God is! God is hope and His word, His promise to never leave me gave me hope for a better day. Through each of these events and many, many more daily life setbacks, I've had to be hopeful and faithful to continue my life's journey. Lean into the invisible power of hope!

Don't give up on life. Don't give up on God. He will never give up on you. Now that is a major reason to be hopeful.

Hope encourages when there is despair. Hoping for the good leads to that good. Hope is a positive life force, an energy that acts as a guiding light in the darkness. Follow it!

Hope enlightens us in the midst of the storms of life. Foster your own and others' hope muscle – seek God's guidance. Seek His will and act accordingly. Your outcome will be positive and successful. His will will come to pass even when you cannot see it in the present moment. Hope is an internal spirit action. Where there is hope, there is action to will through the fog, the wrong, the bad of life's daily challenges. Have hope and share hope with the world around you – every day! Ask your children about hope. What are their hopes?

Ask them about the lack of hope. Have they ever felt hopeless? It is important to share your own story of hope with your children. What could you do as a family to bring hope to others?

"The LORD is my portion, saith my soul; Therefore will I hope in him."
Lamentations 3:24.

Record your reflections here.

Day 10

Love

Oh my God! God is love.

All of life's existence comes from the love of God! He first loved us so He created us. He created the very life we all have within our bodies, our life's house. He commands and expects us to love Him back. He commands us to love others, even when we don't like someone.

What is love and what does it look like to you? Only you can answer this question for yourself. My answer comes from the Word of God and from my own life experiences. A couple of points to cause you to define love for yourself and to share that love with others:

- God is love! I love God!
- My momma was love.
- My daddy loved me.
- I love my son.
- I love life.
- I love my family.

- I love the beauty that God has created:
  - Existence
  - The Earth and all its nature
- I love music.
- I love peace.
- I love my friends and neighbors.
- I love love, righteousness, peace, and joy.
- I love so much more...

For me, love is spiritual. Love is emotional. Love is a positive feeling. Love is a wonderful thought. Love is a choice! I encourage you to choose love – every day!

Day 11

Life

A gift from God.

In the beginning, God created life and I believe He created all things – including each of us, past, present, and future.

Life itself is a spiritual energy force. Life resides in a physical body, and in the spirit within our earthly presence. We are to honor, cherish, nourish, nurture, multiply, give, receive, foster, and love life. Life is breath given to us by God.

We have been gifted with an existence! Yet, in the eternal scheme of time, our lifetime is but "a vapor," as found in James 4:14. We are only physically alive for a very brief moment in time. This being true, we are to live life and not take it for granted. This means we are not to senselessly, randomly kill life.

I pray for you, the reader of this text, that you honor, respect, cherish, value, and live life with reverence to God, His gift to you!

"Let life live – every day."

Day 12

Cultural Competency

*Existing in peace with respect for each
other and respecting the life, the story of
another person is cultural competency.*

In order to live in peace, we must let life live! We must respect each person's God-given gift of life itself. The right for another human to exist in the space and time in which they are born as they are created by God.

Respect for life is a key aspect and belief that we must personally have and share with others. Receive in your spirit, in your heart and mind that each person's life is to be valued and allowed to continue to be alive, without harm, until they naturally pass away, regardless of that person or that group of people's background, ethnicity, nationality, belief system, or lifestyle.

We do not have the right to take away someone's God-given gift of life. If people are not attempting to end your life, you should not do anything to take away their life. It's that simple. We can coexist without gun violence and war. Our life existence depends on everyone adopting this basic and simple belief. Don't overcomplicate our respective right to live!

Day 13

Values

A belief system that drives people to behave,
act, and think in a particular way of being.

Values are a set of ideas, thoughts, beliefs, principles, and standards of operating on a daily basis. Each of these points are developed and shaped by our parents, society, culture, faith, religion, and people we interact with. These ways of thinking, believing, and living can be wonderfully and powerfully positive.

Unfortunately, our values and systems of living in this world with others can also be incredibly dangerous to the continuation of another person's life. We all need to check our values, our ways of thinking and behaving. I believe everything we do, everything that has been created begins with a thought. God thought to create life. Eve thought to eat from the tree of knowledge. Cain thought to kill his brother Abel.

Ever since these early thoughts, our actions have been affected by what we think. This being true, after we have a thought, we act. We do. This thought-to-action pathway can produce positively great things and it can produce horribly negative, ugly things. Like the taking of another innocent human's life. Stop, people. Please stop and grab hold (control) of your thoughts and actions.

Dos and don'ts:

- Do think positive, life-saving, giving, improving thoughts and actions.
- Don't have life-ending, hateful, evil, wrong thoughts and actions.

Yes, it can be that easy (or simple) to make and take the right course of action between life and death. The power of life and death are in the tongue. This thought-to-action pathway can and should be controlled by each of us – every day!

What thoughts do you notice about yourself? Are your thoughts positive? Do you assume goodwill, or do you jump to the negative? Spend some time reflecting on this for yourself and with your children.

Day 14

Humanity

*Is our life form. The mind, body, soul, and
spirit of a person. God's physical creation of
mankind, all of God's created people.*

Humanity is the entire world of people. We, as people, did not create ourselves or another person. This action of creation belongs to God. Yes, He told us to be fruitful and multiply to populate the earth. He gave us our being and our physical organic ability to form life. Yet, it is He who creates life and gives life. He also can take life away. These two primary acts are His job, not ours.

It is not our job to take life nor to take humanity for granted. Life is to be valued beyond our understanding. God gives us breath and it is He who takes our breath away. Let life live mankind!

As you meditate on this word, humanity, today on the calendar of life, stop and give reverence to the humanity of life itself. What an awesome gift from God. Treat life in this manner and make our world a better place for all of us!

Day 15

Patience

*God has been instilling patience – waiting, slowing
down, in me all my life. He's still working on
me – I'm 60+ years old! Patience is golden.*

What is patience? This concept, this virtue means to wait, endure, persevere through. This wait can be difficult for many of us because we live in our own time frame of, I want whatever now! Thus, our challenge. God's time is often not ours. Many of us want what we want when we want it. This usually means immediately. Rarely do we get exactly what we want when we want it.

Waiting, as difficult as it may be, is often more right for us than wrong. To get us through this period of want/need it now, we must endure. We must be diligent as we wait. We must continue on. We must persevere. Eventually, if God so wills, we will have what we want/need.

In the Book of Proverbs, this principle of patience is described as a virtue we must nurture and possess. All throughout our lives, we will continually need to strengthen our patience muscle. This may be especially true when faced with conflict, challenge, or a problematic life decision. I encourage you to respond with patience. Do not act quickly or without thought of the consequences of your actions.

Our life-ending choice to kill is not a reversible action. This is 100 percent true! Only God can give, take, and give life again and again. Life is not a video game. We don't get a second or third chance to "power up." Once we lose patience and take life, the "game" ends! We or the person are then G.O.N.E. This acronym stands for <u>Great One No longer Exists</u>!

Be patient in conflict. De-escalate. Walk away and live to go home. Live another day.

Day 16

Effective Communication

Understand and receive a message
with clarity and purpose.

Each of the preceding words and the words to follow are daily suggestions and actions to incorporate into your day; so is effective communication. Communication involves listening, speaking, and interpreting what is said.

We should seek understanding and to be understood, whether we are texting, gesturing, writing, or making some type of speech. Our ability to communicate effectively may be our best tool to resolve and avoid conflict. Communication will allow us to de-escalate a situation peacefully, long before the moment turns to gun violence or any other form of life-taking violence.

Clarity of our intended message is extremely important in our everyday life. Each interaction with another God-created human is important. Take some time to learn how to manage your anger. Take thought (fore-thought) to control your tongue before the need arises. What you say and how you say it matters. Our tone of voice and body language speak volumes. My mom shared a poem with me when I was a child. As a child, the bass in my voice changed around eight years old. When I was angry, mad, or upset, try as I might to temper myself, the tone and volume of my voice gave me away. Which may have led to a spanking or a timeout, usually a spanking. Thank you, Momma, for teaching me to be aware of how I communicate.

Learning this lesson of managing and controlling my tongue and tone has helped me improve my human relations. I'm not always success-ful with my speech and communication, but this is a method I truly endorse to help produce positive, life-continuing outcomes when dealing with bias, prejudice, dislike of another, distrust, or hatred. Managing these behaviors can be the difference between a violent and non-violent interaction with others.

The Tone of Voice

It's not so much what you say
As the manner in which you say it;
It's not so much the language you use
As the tone in which you convey it.
"Come here," I said.
He looked and smiled.
And straight to my lap he crept.
Words may be mild and fair
But the tone may pierce like a dart;
Words may be soft as the summer air
But the tone may break my heart.
For words come from the mind
Grow by study and art;
But tone leaps from the inner self
Revealing the state of the heart.
Whether you know it or not,
Whether you mean or care.
Gentleness, kindness, love and hate,
envy, anger, are there.
Then, would you quarrels avoid
And peace and love rejoice?
Keep anger out of your words,
Keep it out of your voice.

–Author Unknown

Day 17

Self-Esteem

*Healthy self-esteem is having an accurate and
balanced self-view. This simply means how
good or bad you feel about you. How do you
"see" yourself – your inner and outer self?*

I grew up with my mom and my two older sisters. My mom worked
three jobs at once during a period of our childhood. While she fostered
love and care in me and my sisters, I struggled with my physical size. I
was short and skinny and I hated it. As I began to grow and perform
in sports and academics, I grew out of self-disdain and into being a
more confident person. Having my mom nurture me and tell me I was a
great son no matter my size and that I was a child of God increased my
self-esteem.

We each need a parent, sibling, relative, or friend to help us develop a
positive self-image. Some kids may not have the blessing of a parent in
the home or a loving mentor. They may be in foster care, for example.
You can develop a relationship with a child in this situation. Become
a mentor.

A positive, trustworthy person in a person's (child or adult) life can help improve our world, one person at a time. There's value in each one, teach one. The village model is fluid and has a dynamic impact on helping us feel and see ourselves, and others, in a more positive way. Our positive self-esteem helps us value our lives and the lives of other people.

Your thoughts? Record your reflections here.

Day 18

Righteousness, Peace, and Joy (RPJ)

These three words are my life's mantra,
my guiding light, my compass.

These three words (like Stevie Wonder's song – I love you – these three words) have been a daily way of seeking God, living more like Jesus wants me to be and respecting His plans for me in my relationships with all people. I'm not perfect; no one is, nor will ever be. RPJ helps keep me grounded, happy overall, and respectful of God and life itself.

I hope this inspires you to develop you own life mantra. Your light unto your feet along the path of life. You can adopt mine if you choose. At least until you come up with your own.

In no way do I see myself, nor should you see yourself, as more righteous than another person. Self-righteousness can be a negative if not based on God's guiding spirit. I am in search of God's righteousness for my life. The right path that leads to my salvation eternal, for His peace in my spirit and soul. His joy and happiness in my daily life, as I live and breathe amongst His creation – man, woman, and child!

Take time to discuss this with your kids. Get their thoughts and feedback. What words do you want to live by? Ask your kids to create their own. What is your life's mantra/guiding light?

Day 19

Morality

Is the extent to which an action is right or
wrong, as defined by a believer of Jesus Christ.
What are right and wrong behaviors and beliefs
from our personal perspective affects others.

I am a Christian! I've received God's gift of salvation and I believe Jesus Christ is the son of God. I've accepted Jesus as my personal savior for all of eternity! This belief is what I base my understanding of what is right and wrong behavior – one human to another. This guiding light is the compass that I previously spoke about as being the basis of my understanding of morality. The right things I am to do for my family, myself, my neighbor, and all people are based on this.

Starting with the Ten Commandments and based on my gun violence prevention platform, I am following commandment number six: "thou shall not kill" (Exodus 20:13). I pray that I and all of us will not face the threat of being killed or the decision to kill in defense of our own lives.

To help with these choices and situations, I choose not to kill a person. Not killing humans, in my morality, is the right thing today. Let life live! I believe each human has an innate sense of right and wrong, good and bad. Yes, as we grow up and develop into mature, responsible, life-respecting people, we further our moral compass of right and wrong. Our inborn nature convicts us when we do right and when we do wrong.

I pray we all choose to do right and not kill another person. The choice is ours to make. Choose wisely based on your morality. Can you define your moral compass, your sense of right and wrong? Discuss this with your children. If you have a younger child, ask him/her what is right and what is wrong. One suggestion is to guide this discussion by referring to scriptures. Record your thoughts and reflections below.

Day 20

Kindness

I love this word, this action! What a beautiful
idea to be nice, good, kind to someone.
Kindness makes everyone's day better.

Be kind! Share love, a smile, a friendly word, a hug. Be considerate toward others and watch the love, the goodness spread. Kindness is powerful. Kindness changes us for the better – inside and out. Start with a smile, or hello, an unmistakable gesture to help a fellow human have a better day than they were having before the two of you encountered each other.

Ask your child what one thing he/she can do today to be kind. Develop a kindness plan for the day as a family and revisit this often. Intentional kindness should be modeled for your kids. For instance, you could help a senior take her groceries to the car or you can pay for the car behind you in the drive-through line. Then ask your kids to come up with something they can actually do to be kind, like taking an apple to school for the teacher.

Brainstorm an Intentional Kindness Plan for your family. Use the template to capture your thoughts.

CHOOSE KINDNESS

INTENTIONAL KINDNESS WEEKLY PLANNER

Record an activity for your family to complete each day.

MONDAY

Example: Take the neighbor's trash out.

TUESDAY

WEDNESDAY

THURSDAY

FRIDAY

SATURDAY

SUNDAY

Day 21

God

Maker, creator of Heaven and Earth and all
things within. The Almighty. I am. Adonai.
Sovereign. Omnipotent. Omnipresent. Omniscient.
Alpha and Omega. Our Father. All. Him.
And so much more that words cannot define
or describe. Genesis 1 is applicable here.

Who is He to you?

Day 22

Jesus

*Son of God. My Lord and Savior. The Way, the Truth,
and the Life. Merciful King. Salvation's Holy Light.*

Your thoughts:

Day 23

Holy Ghost/Spirit

Comforter sent to us by Jesus to live
in us and with us every day.

God's holiness spirit given to us to lead us to be more like Jesus – every day. Holy Ghost/Spirit is loving, kind, compassionate, and willing beyond understanding to obey God's commandments toward all of His creation.

Holy Ghost/Spirit is our friend, our guide to living in a righteous way. Holy Ghost/Spirit leads us from within. Some may call Him our conscience that convicts us when we go astray. Holy Ghost/Spirit is God's spiritual energy force living inside us and with us. Listen to Holy Ghost/Spirit inside of you and your life's path will be that of peace and love, not hatred and violence.

He is our comforter, our way maker, our messenger from God and Jesus (Father and Son), our Lord. Holy Spirit advocates for us to live our lives to become more like Jesus within our society, our homes, and our relationships with other humans.

Holy Spirit is in the very breath we breathe. Receive God's given Holy Spirit and continue to live as He guides you. Proverbs 3:5-6 is applicable here: "Trust in the Lord with all thine heart; and lean not unto thine own understanding. In all thy ways acknowledge him, and he shall direct thy paths."

Reflect on the scripture and record what it means to you.

Day 24

Service

Our physical and emotional actions
to help others – every day.

Our doing step! Each day, we are to live out our lives as believers that God/Jesus/Holy Spirit wants us to do goodwill toward His people. This includes not killing each other. He said for us to be our brother's keeper. He said we are to feed His sheep – we the people are His sheep (metaphorically). Serving others blesses others. Are you serving?

Helping others means giving your service to assist another. Time, talents, and your tenth are actions you can take to be helpful on a daily basis. Try giving of yourself and watch your helpful ways have their impact and effect on the world. 1 John 3:18 says, "My little children, let us not love in word, neither in tongue; but in deed and in truth." This is a call to action (to serve) and what God expects our loving words and actions to look like.

Serving others can take many different forms. It can be as simple as calling a relative or friend to check in, or it could be volunteering at a homeless shelter. What does service look like for you and your family? Chat with your children and ask them how they would like to serve. Record your discussion here, then develop an action plan to bring the service project for your family into reality. Start small, but do start.

Day 25

Grace and Mercy

*Often as I was growing up, I would hear my
elders describe grace and mercy as such: "Grace
is God's way of forgiving us for what correction
we deserve, and mercy is Him not giving us
what we do deserve when we do wrong."*

W e should give grace and mercy to each other – even when we may
not deserve to receive them. Grace and mercy are loving kindness offered
to another person as an act of goodwill and forgiveness when that person
falls short of being perfectly righteous. Yes, grace and mercy should be
given even when we are hurt by the actions, attitudes, and behaviors done
against us. Is this easy to do? I say no, it is not easy to do, but it is the right
thing to do to keep peace and to allow each person to continue to live.

I struggle with allowing someone to harm, hurt, or bother me, yet as I
pray my way through those temporary moments of discomfort, I often
find a way to offer my version of grace and mercy to the offending
person. Try this act of grace and mercy in your daily life with your children, spouse, family, friends, neighbors, and the strangers you encounter.

Model grace and mercy and watch the invisible power contained in these two faith-based principles have their effect. Grace and mercy will lead our interactions toward more positive, loving, and respectful life-continuing outcomes!

Day 26

Let Go

Surrender to God – not to your flesh. Deny
thyself and follow God's plan for your life.
His commandments are still relevant.

This act of letting go, of surrendering all to God is critical. This action we take to submit ourselves to God's will may be the most difficult action of our lives. Yet it is the most rewarding thing we will ever do!

Surrender leads to salvation. Surrender leads to loving self and others.

Surrender leads to peace within and beyond ourselves. Surrender leads to forgiveness of self and others. Surrender leads to joy within.

Surrender is not weakness. Surrender is God's strength in us, in every aspect, experience, and encounter we will ever have. Once we surrender, we find strength!

Release your desire to have control over self and others to God's plan for life. This act of surrender begins as you awake from your sleep every day.

It is to continue throughout each day, each breath you take.

Yes, this act of surrender may seem impossible. Impossible to be perfect at surrendering. You are correct. It is if we try to do so by ourselves – alone. Surrender is possible with God. Try it and see another you, a better you!

Day 27

Prayer

A spiritual and verbal communication with
God through Jesus and the Holy Spirit.

Prayer serves innumerable purposes. There is always a reason to pray (Thessalonians). Pray to give thanks. Thanks for all that is good in life, and for your life. Pray to improve all things that are not good at the present in your life. Pray for others:

- Spouse
- Children
- Family
- Neighbors
- Enemies
- World leaders
- Pastors
- Everyone – eight billion souls

When I was a boy, the old folk would often say, "there's power in prayer and prayer changes thangs." They are right.

One of my inspirations for offering *31 Days of Surrender* comes from the weekly, monthly, and yearly calendar that we use to plan our lives by. There's a "day" for many things and people under the sun. We have International Women's Day, Father's Day, Mother's Day, and Grandparents' Day, just to name a few. These are great days to celebrate, but God placed in my spirit to share with you that, in addition to one day of prayer as marked on the annual calendar, we need 31 days of surrendered thinking, behavior, and honoring. Honor God, family, and His creation every day, not just on a designated day on the calendar. Incorporate prayer, God, Jesus, Holy Spirit, kindness, peace, and love into your day – every day.

This daily act of surrender will have an amazing impact and effect on our lives. What do you think? Is this something you can do? Do you agree that this is something you should do? If not, why? Record your thoughts here.

Day 28

Praise and Worship

Glorifying, lauding, and giving
thanks and gratitude unto God.

Express yourself with reverence for the awesomeness of God. Talk to God. Dance and sing to God. Listen for His voice. All of these and more are ways to praise God. How do you show your respect, your thanks, your praise to God?

I enjoy music and my motorcycle as often as I can. When I ride, I listen to music. When I listen to music, I praise God. When I ride, I praise God. I thank Him for His favor, and I thank Him for His beautiful creation (land, air, and sea). I thank Him for a safe ride so I can continue living with my son and my family, enjoying the animals He created. I thank Him for my health, my friends, and my resources. I thank Him for life itself; I can continue doing His will. I thank Him for much more. I thank him for empowering me to write this book.

Pray, praise, and worship God – every day.

Day 29

Trust and Believe

*When I trust, I surrender to a fact, a truth that what
is said is true beyond a doubt. When I believe, I trust
that word, that truth, that action that leads to an "is."
This "is" is a definite? No doubt. We can trust God!*

Who else can you trust?

Do you trust yourself?

How can you develop trust?

Are you trustworthy?

Talk to your kids about trust. What does it mean to be trustworthy?

Day 30

Self-Love

Do you love yourself?
*Please refer to number 10 (Love) to help
you answer this question of self-love.

I believe we must first love God in order to have a healthy, spiritual self-love of ourselves. Since He created us, we are to honor Him by loving His creation – ourselves! There are many ways to express self-love for the temple God created which is you!

Practice your definition, your belief of what it means in the eyes of God to love yourself. Here are a few more words and thoughts to help you know if you are practicing self-love in a God-honoring way:

1. Love is not vain.
2. Love is not puffed up.
3. Love is not arrogance or conceit.
4. Love is humble.
5. Love is peaceful.
6. Love is caring.

7. Love is time.
8. Love is giving.
9. Love is respecting your life, your temple.
10. Love values life.

What ways can you show self-love? What ways can your kids show self-love? Record your ideas below.

Day 31

Humility

*To humble oneself suggests not being prideful,
arrogant, or hateful. Humility implies the ability
to love outwardly first! Reverence, with awe,
for the fact that we did not create ourselves.*

All our good things come from God, our supreme creator and authority. Being humble recognizes that we are not gods. We are humans created by God to serve the life plan He has for us, which helps everyone live for the greater good.

We exist because He created us – not ourselves. This belief humbles me and hopefully you.

Final Thoughts

These thirty-one words can be read and meditated upon through each of the thirty-one days of every month. Yes, even those months with 28, 29, or 30 days – Selah. As the days of life's calendar turn forward (not backward), I encourage you to reflect on every word or phrase listed here continually.

Place them all, or your favorite one, on your calendar, phone, on your desk at work or in your office, or on the mirror in your bathroom. Let the power of God and positive affirmations help make life better for you and every human on the planet.

Part Two

RESPECTING LIFE EVERY DAY

Respecting Life
Every Day

The preceding pages dealt with 31 reflections. You have spent time in prayer, meditation, and discussion. You undoubtedly invited your children into these moments in order to help them develop a better understanding of what it means to live a life where hate is surrendered.

In this section of the book, I will delve deeper into a few topics. It is my hope that you will read, reflect, and engage with your children. The use of the village model could lead to a more peaceful world. This is my reason for discussing it in this section of the book. Once the village model is in place, it is of utmost importance that we make sure younger generations truly understand these important topics:

- Making the right decisions
- Managing anger
- Thinking beyond what you see
- Understanding de-escalation techniques
- Knowing what it means to let life live

- Understanding what hate is and how to stand against it
- Resolving conflict peacefully

Once these areas are explored, you and your children will be equipped to surrender hate and live peacefully.

One

The Village Model

The phrase "it takes a village to raise a child" is an African proverb that conveys the message that it takes many people (a village) to provide a safe and healthy environment for children. Going back to when I was a child, this was the model in which my sisters and I were raised. My mother worked hard and everyone within the community sort of looked out for one another. If you were caught misbehaving or being disrespectful, an adult would step in immediately. It was hard for us to get away with anything growing up. There was always an extra set of eyes and ears on us, whether we liked it or not. Unlike today, where you can scroll through any of the popular social media platforms and see tons of videos of children telling their parents what to do. I'm not judging...I'm only making mention to show how times have changed.

In case you didn't know, I grew up as a little country boy. Whenever my friends would have a disagreement, we would duke it out (wrestle) or take a break from speaking to one another for a day or two and that was as far as it would go. For the most part, we knew how to control our emotions. Our small conflicts never boiled over into serious disagreements. Somehow, we understood the importance of taking a step back to calm down. The next day, we were back outside playing together as if nothing ever happened. Learning how to resolve differences without using violence was the result of being raised under the village model. When arguments and fights would break out, adults would use this as a teachable moment. Unbeknownst to us, we were being taught how to resolve conflict in a healthy and positive manner. The adults would ask us questions like, "How would you like it if Tommy just took your bike and brought it back with a flat tire? How would that make you feel?" The adults would enforce consequences that caused us to take responsibility for our actions. In the case of the bike with the flat tire, we might have to pay to fix the flat using our own money.

Children living in the 21st century could truly benefit from "it takes a village". Part of what makes the village model effective is the support and guidance others provide to families living within the community. The village model is made up of the following people:

- Parents
- Older siblings
- Extended family members
- Neighbors
- Teachers
- Community members
- The church

There are some things I learned as a child that have affected me into adulthood. This is one of them. I was introduced to hunting at a very early age. Having access to shotguns and rifles at such a young age was more like a rite of passage for me; however, I was never left unattended while using the gun. An adult was always present to ensure no harm came to me or to others. I was around 13 when I came face to face with a nest of hungry baby birds waiting for their feeding. If I remember correctly, there were four baby birds in the nest. It was then that I realized how one bullet claimed the lives of not one but five birds. There was no way the baby birds could survive without the aid and protection of their mother. Witnessing what had taken place gave me a different perspective on life and what it meant to be among the living.

We now live in a society where empathy and compassion for human life have become almost obsolete. If we are serious about surrendering hate, we must take human life seriously. No one wants to die young! My guess is that no one wants to spend the rest of their lives incarcerated for taking a life as well. Just as my family taught me what it meant to use a gun responsibly, we must make sure our children know what this means. Mommas and dads, please instill this belief and life-respecting approach in your children. This is one answer to how we prevent and stop gun violence in our communities – in this lifetime! Give God His sovereign power back. This power of life and death belongs to Him, not us.

One more story on this idea of the impact of the village model, a loving parent, church family, and my own intuition. While mowing my yard as a young man, engaged to be married and planning to start a family after getting married, I heard a voice in my spirit telling me to break the chain, the curse of absentee fatherhood, of a poverty mindset and the continual path to incarceration and deadly violence. What a revelation! I committed at that moment that I would not be an absentee dad, that I would work to take care of my wife and child and guide my child (my eventual son) on how to live his life. This included a healthy dose of obedience to his mom and I, to look to God for guidance and get a college-level education, and to learn how to interact with others to avoid violent, illegal, and deadly outcomes. This voice in my spirit (God) has continued to guide me, even during my sin and mistakes! Without my mom, sisters, cousins, aunts, uncles, and my faith in God, I may have continued the family/life curse of negative behaviors and bad choices that would have passed on to my son, his children and so on. The village model and many other inspirations have helped me become a productive messenger for God, my family, my community, and hopefully for each of you. It's okay to follow a better life path for yourself, your family, friends, and for each member of this human race. Join me and many others like me in breaking this curse, this chain of violence toward self and others in each of its forms. Make the decision, right now, to discontinue the negative, hateful, evil, and violent behaviors that may be in your family bloodline. You and God can do this! You have the power and strength to save lives – yours, your family, and the members of the village of which you are a member. Each one, teach one is the idea I'm suggesting to you.

I would like to define the village model as I see it.

Defining the Village Model

Love thy neighbor equals more peace, less violence, and more respect for life.

1. **God:** The creator of us all. Psalms 100:5 states, "For the Lord is good; his mercy is everlasting; and his truth endureth to all generations."

2. **Family:** The family is the foundational institution of society ordained by God. God created a system for us to have harmony, unity, and community.

3. **Respect for Life:** There's a living, breathing soul and spirit created by God for each living individual. If you have some level of respect for your own life, you should have respect for another human life.

4. **Morals:** Your belief system; the development of one's behavior and understanding of right and wrong shapes how you interact with others. A productive society cannot exist without morals.

5. **Values:** Positive life! Positive living! Your values should reflect positive life and living.

Two

Change Comes from Right Decisions

Once the village is in place, it supports individuals. Ultimately, individuals have to make their own decisions. These decisions can either contribute to a harmonious, peaceful world or tear down the world. The choice we make after careful consideration is a *decision*. Unfortunately, some young people aren't getting the guidance they need to know how to make the right decisions. One of my goals for this book is to empower you, the parent, to help your child understand how to make sound decisions and to share the importance of having a plan in place, so if they ever face an unsettling, potentially life-altering situation, they are prepared to defuse the situation, walk away, and live another day.

It begins with the positioning of right versus wrong. From a young age, we begin learning the difference between what's right and what's wrong.

A right choice could save a life, while a wrong choice could end a life. Keep in mind, decision making can be subjective. Everyone's upbringing isn't the same and not everyone shares the same values or outlook on life. It all boils down to the decision maker him/herself.

In today's world, it is imperative that we begin to teach our children the importance of decision making so that they can understand the potential consequences and results of their actions. While teaching values like honesty and respect, I also taught my son the significance of right thoughts, right attitude, right actions, and right behavior. Each principle empowered him to make positive life choices regarding his physical well-being and those around him. If for some reason he doubted his decision, his mother and I provided plenty of guidance. We created a loving environment, which meant he felt he could openly discuss his decision making without fear of condemnation. As parents, it is our responsibility to provide children with the skills necessary to make healthy decisions that could ultimately save their life.

To illustrate the point further, here are a few scenarios.

If your child hangs out with the wrong crowd, the following may occur. The child may:

- Steal cars
- Break into someone's home
- Participate in armed robbery
- Carry a concealed weapon
- Get involved in gang-related activity

This all could lead to a conviction, time being incarcerated, or experiencing and witnessing negative, traumatic events.

How can you help prevent your child from participating in these events?

You can help lay a foundation that includes teaching him/her how to make the right decisions based on biblical principles. Read the Bible to your child when he/she is young, and as they grow have them read to you. Discuss what the scriptures mean and offer personal applications. Make time to read on a consistent basis.

Three

Thinking Beyond
What You See

Managing Anger and Giving Grace

Being able to make good decisions involves having the ability to manage your anger effectively. Many angry people have reacted out of pure emotion and made decisions that altered the rest of their lives in very negative ways. One of the golden rules is to treat others the way we want to be treated. To better understand how this rule can be practiced and implemented, we should ask ourselves how it is that we as individuals can interact with other human beings, especially when we have our own prejudices, biases, and life experiences. How do we want to be treated by others? Certainly, if we have these biases and prejudices, others must have them as well, correct? Keep in mind, our cultural background could play a role in how we see ourselves and how we choose to treat others.

As simple as the "golden rule" may sound, I don't believe that people can arrive at this place without looking within first. When we internally reflect on who we are and what we need, grace appears. Offering grace is what I would like to inspire, and what I believe people can achieve if we "conduct ourselves toward others as we would have them act towards us." -Aristotle

This brings me to the passage in 1 Corinthians 13:11, "When I was a child, I spake as a child, I understood as a child, I thought as a child: but when I became a man, I put away childish things." All this is true, and if we take a minute to understand, we realize that that we are *not* forever who we were. There is room for change; the only requirement is that we choose to change and then become an agent of change. An agent of change is someone who supports a new course of action. The responsibilities of a change agent are to think beyond what is seen, beyond skin tone, hair texture, languages, cultural differences, and ethnicity. When we become people-focused, we can extend grace to one another freely. Offering grace to another can be interchanged with forgiveness that starts with "self." We hear over and over again about the importance of forgiving others, but how often are we reminded to forgive ourselves? The more you practice giving grace to yourself, the better you feel and the more open you become with extending that same grace to others. Why? Because no one ever questions if they've experienced grace; people know it when they receive it.

How to Give Grace

There must be a plan in place for how we treat others if our goal is to surrender hate by extending grace. Extending grace is something you are able to do if you know how to effectively manage your anger.

One of my best teaching moments was when I taught my son how to manage his anger. As his father, I had a responsibility to teach him, as a young black male, how to be responsible with his emotions. Anger is something we all must learn to control. I explained that if he were ever angry or upset with his parents, a classmate, or even a friend, he was not allowed to transfer that anger onto the next person. Since anger is an expression of frustration, I also taught him that it was important for him to understand what he was really angry about and to identify who he was angry with. Anger is a natural human emotion that needs to be tamed. It is our responsibility as parents to equip our kids with skills that empower them to manage their emotions, particularly anger. We should teach them early, then guide them as they grow. This teaching guided my son throughout his life, and it has worked for me as well. Imagine how much better things would be if everyone taught their kids how to manage their emotions and control their anger.

Anger can make you feel as if you're losing control, but when there's a plan in place you can take control of your anger before it takes control of you. In return, you can walk away from potentially conflicting, negative, and violent interactions. The key is to already have a strategic plan for how you will behave. Your life may depend on you knowing how to de-escalate a situation to live another day. De-escalation puts you on the right side, peaceful side, good side, and grace side of the situation. When we are positioned on the right side, it offers an opportunity for us to pass more grace into the world. With over eight billion people on this planet we call Earth, the magical question is, how is it that we make it home safely to wake up and start anew the next day? We need to have a plan for ourself, others, and all life.

Parents, develop a plan (agreement) to help your child create and give grace. A plan is presented below. Discuss it with your children.

How to Think Beyond What You See

1. The Golden Rule

Treat others the way you want to be treated. My upbringing taught me to be friendly if I wanted to have friends. I was asked to treat people like I preferred to be treated. This meant to me that if I wanted people to treat me nicely and kindly, then I would need to do the same to them. If I wanted friends, I needed to be friendly toward others. Simple, right? The Golden Rule asks us to do unto others as we would have them do unto us. If you don't like to be yelled at and called bad names, then don't do so to others. We teach people how to treat us and they teach us how they want to be treated.

2. Resolve Conflict Effectively

Resolve means come to an agreement. When interacting with others, these agreements need to be mutual. Mutual agreements help conflicting situations end without violence and/or hurt feelings. Taking a win-win approach when you have a disagreement with someone leads to a positive outcome. This positive outcome leads to an effective end result between people. The actions you take to positively find a mutual agreement when you are presented with a potentially negative outcome can lead to an effective, *everyone gets to go home safely,* outcome!

3. Keep Your Tone and Voice Neutral

I think I can say, for the majority of people, that most people don't like to be yelled at or spoken to with an angry, *I don't like you,* tone of voice. This being the case, we should not speak to others with an angry, threatening voice whenever we communicate with another. All our voices have the capacity to increase or decrease the volume of our words and sounds. The old directive from parents to use your inside voice is a good way to speak to a person when you are attempting to avoid or minimize an angry situation.

4. **Avoid Overreacting**

Ever met someone who is an alarmist? Or a person who lives their life at a level 10 on a 10-point scale? Responses to another person who may be attempting to cause you harm that are out of line with the situation often lead to an argument/disagreement. Be conscious of how you react to a situation. Don't be overly alarmed, but you should be situationally aware of the moment and the encounter with each person.

5. **Make Wise Choices**

Wise choices minimize problems! Making a choice to not get involved in illegal activity is a wise choice. The Book of Proverbs, mostly written by King Solomon (often considered one of the wisest men ever), is a great source to help you identify and understand what a wise choice looks like. Read the entire chapter and discuss it with your child. I'm sure you have faced a situation that required you to make a choice between right and wrong. It is my belief that we are born with a sense of right and wrong, good, and bad, cold and hot. The experiences we have, coupled with wisdom gained from the Bible, our parents, relatives, and friends, help us make right, good, and wise choices.

6. **Respect Others' Space**

Some of us enjoy close physical contact with our family, friends, spouse, and children. This may not be true for our encounters with people we don't know. Until you know for sure that a person is not intending to cause you harm, a good rule of thumb in the self-defense community is to keep distance between you and the other person. A physical, not touching contact distance of one to three feet apart provides you with enough time to react accordingly if the encounter becomes threatening. Personally, I don't like to be close enough to a person to smell their breath.

7. **Seek to Understand**

   How do you seek to understand a person? I seek to understand a person by listening and observing. Listen to what they are saying and pay attention to their body movements. Are their words threatening, or are they kind and gentle? Are their movements slow and deliberate, or are they abrupt or aggressive? Paying attention to what a person is saying and how they are behaving will help you gain an understanding of their intentions – good or bad.

8. **Actively Consider Other People's Perspectives**

   Gaining an understanding of another person and their story (situation) allows you an opportunity to gain a positive or negative gut feeling about them. Listening, being empathetic, and having compassion help you accept differing perspectives. Opening up your viewpoint to another person's understanding on a particular subject can help resolve conflict. Being open to another's perspective may enlighten you to the day-to-day challenges that everyone faces. We each have a story (life experience) that is different than another's.

De-escalation Techniques

In my view, to be effective at conflict resolution one must also include the skill of de-escalation. Learning how to manage conflict includes some key elements, as does learning de-escalation techniques. De-escalation simply means preventing potential violence.

1. **Say It Politely**

   I'm sure you've heard the old saying of "it's not what you say but how you say it" before, right? Well, this statement is a key component of successful de-escalation. Speaking softly and respectfully are not weaknesses. They are strengths that can and should be learned. Speaking politely to a person who is in a heightened emotional state has a calming, subtle power. Controlling ourself (our tongue) helps ease tension between yourself and another. Help to neutralize volatility and aggression by not speaking angrily.

   Honestly, speaking politely is not easy and it takes practice. Listening to someone berate you or scream at you can set off your internal fight or flight alarm. If you don't control your own anger, you will struggle to help offer a peaceful solution during a potentially dangerous situation. Offer verbal respect when you are being challenged during a discussion. This will help neutralize and calm that situation. Say what you need to say, but say it politely, honestly, and with a calming courage.

2. **Be Respectful**

   How does one be respectful? The previous description of saying things politely is a good place to start. The idea of "how you say what you say" continues to be helpful when offering respectful and potentially differing viewpoints in a contentious conversation. Allow the other person to voice their opinion. Listen. Then, respond with a mild tone of voice but with your truth.

3. **Don't Posture in a Threatening Manner**

   What does this mean? It means don't make aggressive or threatening body movements toward another person. Don't show your displeasure with your physical response. No clenched fists, no reaching for a weapon (gun or knife), don't puff up your chest, don't move in anger toward a person with whom you are in conflict. Don't show the person that you are being aggressive or defensive. Maintain a neutral physical presence. Disengage as necessary. This means to remove yourself from the scenario if you sense aggressive and potentially violent actions may occur (yours or the other person's). Learn to walk away to live another day!

4. **Apologize and Mean It**

How does saying you are sorry make you feel? Does it make you feel soft or weak? Does it make you feel like you've lost? Well, it should not. Saying you are sorry and meaning it should make you feel strong, empowered, empathetic, and righteous. When you apologize, you are offering and seeking forgiveness! Giving and asking for forgiveness has an incredible power to defuse a situation almost immediately. Think about it: when someone tells you that they are sorry, you probably immediately begin to calm down and see things in a different light. Right? If offering or receiving a heartfelt apology doesn't make you or the person you are encountering behave with less aggression, then you should seek to remove yourself from the situation. You may need to seek additional support or further distance from the offending person. This may include seeking the help of a third party (parent, relative, friend, teacher, law enforcement, etc.).

5. **Control Your Anger**

If you are angry and cannot control yourself, the chances you are about to experience a troubling encounter increase exponentially. Gaining control of yourself helps you manage or control the situation you find yourself in. First things first: calm yourself down, understand the consequences of out-of-control behavior and think your way through a mutually positive outcome. There are numerous anger management training courses and equally as many people who are available to assist you with managing your own anger. Anger management is not a simple concept, yet we've all had some experience with learning how to control our own anger. Ask for help from a parent, family member, friend, mentor, or a professional counselor.

Do not lash out in anger! Ask for and seek help. Your life and freedom may depend on how you handle your own anger and the anger directed toward you by another person. Attend a course, a workshop, a training to assist you with techniques to help you reduce your anger response. See www.letlifeliveinc.org as a potential resource to assist you toward positive, life-sustaining outcomes!

6. **Keep Your Hands and Feet to Yourself**
Maintaining distance, speaking politely, and not posturing aggressively are all important techniques to assist you in de-escalation and in avoiding conflict, but so are keeping your hands and feet to yourself! Additionally, do not let someone touch you when they are expressing anger, tension, or conflict. As a 1960s baby, I learned this very early in life, partly because I had two older sisters and boys were taught not to hit girls. I've had "keep your hands to yourself" ingrained into my consciousness since I was a child. Don't hit, kick, or spit on anyone.

Matthew 5:39 says to turn the other cheek if someone strikes you. While I've never been good at that tenet, I have always respected what it teaches. It teaches temperance. It teaches how to avoid escalating an already dangerous situation. It also teaches not to harm another. Admittedly, this is a work in progress for me and perhaps for you. Let's keep working on this command and encourage others to do the same. We now need to include asking people not to shoot each other into this ancient practice that is designed to reduce the amount of conflict between people.

7. **Offer to Pray with the Individual**

A last but first resort in any situation (positive, negative, or potentially violent) is to pray. Pray before you leave your home. Pray before you encounter a person. Pray for a person as you are interacting with them (usually silently). When your spirit tells you that a conflict is arising, ask the person if you can pray with them and for them. Prayer defuses people's anger like no other force! I believe we all know right from wrong and when a person is ready to do wrong to another, there is a moment when they probably question themselves. Is this something I should do? Why am I about to harm this person? Questions like these in the hearts and minds of many people offer the opportunity to intervene and ask the person to think it through. A prayer helps them realize their actions may lead to unwanted consequences for themselves and the person they are about to execute violence upon.

You ask, realistically, will every potentially violent person respond to a person who is praying for them? Probably not. Yet, inserting prayer in a moment of distress may be just what the situation requires for everyone to make it back home safely without further incident and negative consequences. Surrender Your Hate and Let Life Live!

Four

Let Life Live

Let Life Live is a personal pledge recited by participants attending any workshops or trainings I conduct where the message of Surrendering Your Hate is being shared. *Let Life Live* speaks to our differences as a people and the importance of showing and giving respect towards one another. Doing this allows people to agree on the idea that they want life to continue to live – their lives, as well as the lives of others. This example can also be found in the Bible, as the sixth commandment (Exodus 20:13) that forbids direct and intentional killing. Imagine all of humanity consciously deciding to firmly uphold "thou shalt not kill." Now ask yourself, how could a commandment originally given to Moses and the Israelite people by God before Christ reshape the society in which we live today?

I believe that by respecting this faith-based principle, we will work daily in all our interactions with human beings to let them live and help them live. This can be carried out by feeding the hungry, clothing the naked, and sheltering those who are homeless and displaced. This is something you might decide to do as a family by creating your own family service project.

Visit a shelter or take food to the homeless in your city. The goal is for humanity as a whole to discover new ways to de-escalate whatever conflict is around them so everyone can go home safely to live another day. I know firsthand how disagreements and unexplainable challenges can corrupt the hearts and minds of people. I don't say this to find fault in anyone; I am purely sharing from my own personal experiences and understanding.

In order to *Let Life Live,* one cannot permit anger to just run freely. Ephesians 4:26 states, "Be ye angry, and sin not." Anger is an emotion that when unchecked can lead to people lashing out in ways that result in potentially negative and unwarranted outcomes. Let's face it, anger is something that will be with us; however, we should never allow anger to turn into actions that are sinful. Imagine if we were to channel our anger towards something beneficial for all – a renewed heart and mind is a good place to start. Gifting your children with this lesson will prove to be beneficial to them. The earlier they learn to control their anger, the better off they will be.

What I am about to address next may still be on the hearts and minds of many. Before I begin, I sincerely want you to know that I understand and feel pain, even today. I would like to address the senseless death of George Floyd. As I watched the viral video that circulated on May 25, 2020, I felt a strong presence of anger and even hate come over me. My thoughts immediately shifted my focus towards my son. At the time of George Floyd's death, my son was a 22-year-old college graduate beginning his career as an officer in the Marine Corps. As a father, you can't help but think, even if just for a moment, what you would do if it were to happen to your child. My next thought was – it must stop! We (civilization) must do something to ensure that it stops.

It has become dangerous to be among the living. Leaving one's house and interacting with other members of society has the potential of turning violent in an instant. In recent news, I was disturbed by the events of an 18-year-old gunman releasing fire, killing Black people in a grocery store. This type of senseless killing undermines everyone's state of mind and makes people feel unsafe. It becomes a constant undertone, the fear that some hateful, gun-carrying individual who doesn't value life may take your life or your family's life. Is that what we must look forward to? Is this the kind of world we want our children to grow up and live in? I'm imagining that you agree with me in saying this is not what we want. The purpose of this book is to send a direct message to mankind concerning what has been happening in this country and around the globe for far too long. I don't know about you, but I'm fed up – and I'm demanding change.

I grew up in Leesburg, Florida, not far from Sanford, Florida, where a teenage boy's life was taken by a self-appointed neighborhood watcher. This watcher felt his role was that of a simulated police officer. On February 26, 2012, this young man's death inspired a new protest against violence towards Black people and sparked the Black Lives Matter movement. Trayvon Martin was his name.

Five

Hate Is Taught

Making good decisions and managing hate are both effective practices to respect life every day; however, if we are going to really make
a difference and change the world, we should talk about hate. If we
are to raise children that are empowered to surrender hate, they should
understand what it means to be anti-racist. Sadly, children are affected
by discriminatory beliefs and practices at every level. I believe racism is
introduced behind closed doors. I also believe that children are taught
what to love and what to hate, including who to love and who to hate.
The message of love and hate is received at a very young age. I attended an
event where a landowner from South Africa spoke. He shared details of
how he was taught to hate Blacks. He went into excruciating detail about
how taking the life of who he once believed was his enemy was God's
work. As a child, he was taught that killing Blacks was doing the right
thing. The seeds of hate were planted during this man's formative years.

We assume that racism is a personal choice, when in fact it can be learned
early in development, because it is taught to someone by their parents or

the environment in which they were raised. The influence parents have on a child's understanding of race must be discussed, because the goal is to surrender hate. We must push back against the message of hate. I'm not saying it will be easy, but we should put forth the effort if we ever want to see change. Perhaps we begin with dismantling implicit and explicit bias implanted in children from a young age. How do we do this? We start by filling in the knowledge gap. We must first understand who shaped their judgment about others. Research by Shaoying Liu et. al (2015) found that between the ages of six and 12 months, babies begin to show a preference for members of their own racial groups, and within the first year of life children are flooded with messages that shape their thoughts and feelings towards others.[1]

Truth be told, our children are picking up on status hierarchy from the culture we build around them. For instance, imagine a homeless Black man on the street begging for money. What do you as a parent do? Do you set an example by showing compassion, such as giving money or food? Do you simply acknowledge the man's existence? Or do you pretend like you don't see him and ignore his presence? Can showing genuine compassion reprogram a child's beliefs? Is showing compassion the start of creating an understanding and showing respect for others who may be different? This basic principle of respecting all people can go a long way in aiding children to live peacefully.

Surrendering hate may require that we get old school and go back to a grassroots methodology. Meaning getting the government involved. I don't believe legislation can stop hatred, but I do believe in justice! When hatred does manifest, it needs to be corrected. People need to be held accountable; by doing so, it may force violators to examine their own personal beliefs. A campaign such as this could spread worldwide, offering a new perspective on the topic of race in our country. Additionally, there are many issues in our school systems that impact students negatively, such as hate, violence, alcohol and drug use, bullying, and cyberbullying. When the idea of bringing prayer back into our schools is introduced, many take issue. I believe that prayer in schools would help students face these issues and would actually have a positive impact on schools.

Something of this caliber takes a lot of work, but I believe that the work can be done. First thing first, it starts with us! We must become positively contagious against hate in every way. The only way for us to change the message of hate is to challenge it. This includes uprooting negative seeds of influence (what was taught, modeled, and demonstrated at a young age) and replanting new harmonious and peaceful ideas.

We can unteach hate by bringing prayer back to school, engaging governmental agencies to pass legislation that would require all students to participate in conflict resolution, and giving training in violence prevention. Ultimately, each person's heart must change to one of love for others. Local, state, and federal governments can get involved to produce widespread change. School boards can enact policies that promote peaceful, nonviolent ways of being.

Teach your children to have respect for others and humanity. If God created life, God created humanity, and we must show respect to the lives He created. Besides, no one is better than anyone else; from the janitor who sweeps floors to the CEO of a Fortune 500 company, we all represent humanity!

Here are eight ways you can take a personal stance against hate:

1. **Be Prayerful:** Spend time in prayer with your children. Lead them in daily prayers for peace. You can pray for peace in the school, your city, the nation, and the world.

2. **Be Bold:** Teach your child to stand boldly in the face of adversity. Encourage him/her to always seek a peaceful solution to conflict.

3. **Be Respectful:** This idea and action was listed as one of the 31 daily reflections/meditations earlier in the book. As being respectful relates to overcoming hatred, it becomes another key element of valuing human life. Hatred does not value human life! Employ your personal understanding of how you want another person to respect you back towards people who need you to respect them – their humanity, their race, nationality, existence.

4. **Be Understanding:** "If any of you lack wisdom, let him ask of God, that giveth to all men liberally, and upbraideth not; and it shall be given him." James 1:5

   Seeking understanding (wisdom) is a biblical commandment. Jesus said to his disciples, apostles, and followers that they should seek understanding from God the Father through prayer. He will give us understanding through our prayer lives. He does this liberally and He doesn't hold it (understanding) from us. Ask and we will receive. To do all of this, one must want to. Help your child "want" to! Doing so creates a generation of people, going forward, that live the need to understand someone other than themselves. Accepting varying viewpoints and lifestyles, while valuing life itself, will help reduce violence of all sorts (gun, domestic, wars, etc.).

5. **Be a Listener:** Have you ever heard your parent or grandparent say the phrase "listen and learn"? If you have and if you understood what they meant by this little instructional statement, you know that they were offering very wise words to you. They were asking you to hear, to gain an understanding of what views, opinions,

and facts were being shared by whomever the speaker was that was offering you some information. Once you hear and gain an understanding of another person's thinking, you can then respond with more care, kindness, respect, love, empathy, compassion, and so on (see again the reflections in the first part of this book). Try listening first before offering your viewpoint when you find yourself feeling hatred, dislike, or disagreement toward another person.

6. **Be Open:** Don't shut down! Remain open in your thinking. Listening to, understanding, and respecting another person may enlighten you. Hatred clouds our thinking and may lead us to angry, violent, and offensive acts. Having a mindset that allows you to seek peaceful outcomes during each interaction with someone you believe you have a difference, dislike, or hatred for will minimize many of the dangerous outcomes that hate has produced throughout mankind's history.

7. **Be Love:** God is love. Love is the antidote to hate! Give love and you will receive love.

8. **Be Hopeful:** Being hopeful may seem like you are not "doing" anything externally. Being hopeful when we interact with others sets the stage for positive outcomes. If you approach a person-to-person interaction with positive expectations and feelings, you are setting the stage for those positive emotions and outcomes to occur. If you have negative or hateful feelings and expectations, you are also setting the stage for those negative and potentially violent outcomes to happen. Be positively hopeful within yourself to affect your interpersonal relationships. A kind word and a smile go a long way when interacting with many people. Be the light and not the darkness.

Six

Resolving Conflict Peacefully

One of the main reasons I wrote this book was to encourage peaceful conflict resolution. Surrendering hate is a large part of conflict resolution. If the heart is void of hate, it becomes easier to walk away from stressful, tense situations. Conflicts can arise anywhere and at any time. Conflicts can be major or minor. For instance, if you don't like the way the clerk talks to you at the store, it can create conflict, but you can easily ignore the clerk and take your business elsewhere. Alternatively, the conflict may be at your job, where someone may accuse you of something you did not do, question your integrity, or disparage the quality of your work. Conflicts can arise due to personal, political, financial, or emotional differences. When someone decides to mistreat you, screams and yells at you, or threatens bodily harm, it might not be as simple as turning and walking away. What would you do if the conflict was life-threatening? In this section, I will offer practical steps you can take when you encounter conflict. The idea is to familiarize yourself with this and create your own plan so that in the event something happens, you know what to do. Additionally, you may want to review this with your children and have them become familiar with it, as they too may face conflict in and out of school.

Conflict resolution involves resolving differences and reaching peaceful agreements to what could be difficult, potentially violent circumstances. Situations are fluid and ever-changing. There isn't one formula or method that will resolve every conflict satisfactorily for all parties. This is why it is critical to have a conflict resolution mindset or plan in place that can help a cooler head prevail in the midst of chaos. This plan will aid in eliminating negative consequences, violent responses, and dire outcomes.

Resolving conflict peacefully involves:

- Active listening
- Using empathy
- Surrendering hate
- Detaching from negative emotions
- Compromise

Active Listening

When conflict arises, you should start with a willingness to hear what's going on with the other person. Listen without bias, prejudice, or other negative emotions. Express your willingness to resolve differences positively. Some phrases that you can use to communicate your willingness might be: *I hear you, let's work this out, I can understand your point of view,* and *I see how you might think that.*

If you really want to make sense of what the other person is trying to communicate, you should focus on what they are saying instead of on what you want to say in response. Talking while a person is speaking often adds anger and creates miscommunication. If we are to become effective listeners, we should use our ears and eyes more than we use our mouths. The old saying about one mouth and two ears is very relevant when trying to positively resolve conflict and anger, since we should listen more than we speak. Apply the "two or three to one" plan: Listen two to three times more than you talk. Allow the other person to express him/herself. Practice patience and poise while the person is speaking. Lastly, let the person know they have been heard with a head nod or verbal affirmation. You may need to find a peaceful place within yourself during a disagreement or argument. This peace can come from prayer, praise, and patience cultivated on a daily basis. At the beginning and the end of the interaction, you should offer forgiveness and seek to be forgiven to minimize the negative effects of conflicts.

Active listening involves managing your tone, keeping your hands to yourself, monitoring your body language, and maintaining a safe distance between you and the other person. In return, it will help you arrive at a peaceful resolution.

Be aware. Be observant; pay attention to verbal and nonverbal cues. When active listening doesn't seem to work, you may need to seek assistance from family members and close friends. In some instances, if things get critical you may need to engage law enforcement. Always be prepared to leave a situation as quickly as possible, particularly if you feel threatened!

Using Empathy

Empathy requires you to understand another person's feelings and point of view. It may not be easy to have empathy, but it is necessary to surrender hate and resolve conflict peacefully. Having empathy means you have to be willing to be selfless, not selfish. You might have to imagine what it is like to walk in the other person's shoes, be willing to understand, and be relatable. Halpern (1993) defined empathy as "the ability to resonate emotionally with, yet stay aware of, what is distinct about the other's experience. It requires imagination."[2]

This necessitates maturity, wisdom, respect for life, and the old concept of "taking the high road". You should be willing to dismiss the emotional feeling of being disrespected. This creates an exit and allows you to get out of your feelings and let go of your pride.

Let's take the example of the store clerk speaking to you rudely mentioned earlier in this chapter. If you want to show empathy, you might try to determine what is impacting the clerk by engaging him in conversation. Let's say you talk with the clerk and because of your discussion, you learned that he works three jobs in order to take care of his family and he rarely gets to sleep; as a result, he is tired, and this shows in his interactions with the customers. You could show empathy by telling the clerk you can understand why he seems impatient because you too would be tired if you had to work 15-hour days.

It may be difficult to be empathetic if you find yourself in a volatile situation where violent, angry, over the top behavior is occurring and danger is present. Your personal safety should always be top of mind. In some cases, this type of behavior could lead to conflict that erupts into physical altercations, gun violence, and even death. If you express your desire to be nonviolent, this can de-escalate situations in some instances, but this isn't always the case. Conflict involves two or more people, and you may not know the state of mind of the other person. You might need to leave the interaction immediately to preserve your life. Going home safely at the end of the conflict is the ultimate goal for all involved parties. Avoiding death, hospitalization, loss of employment, and/or incarceration are all more positive outcomes.

Surrendering Hate

Ask yourself: are you contributing to hate in society? Are you standing by and ignoring hate or are you actively working to eradicate hate? You don't have to be doing anything big, but are you even doing any small thing? In order to surrender hate, one must first recognize some of the forms of hate. Hate is intense dislike and can be based on fear, lack of understanding, and knowledge. Hate produces strong emotions, and unfortunately hate can spread easily. The very word itself produces negative emotions and energy. Yet, Jesus our Lord and Savior hated a few things and He spoke against those things.

The Charleston Nine were nine church members killed while worshipping at the Emanuel African Methodist Church in Charleston, South Carolina because of hate. This tragic event sparked the #hatewontwin movement, a social media campaign started by the granddaughter of one of the victims of the senseless shooting, Alana Simmons. She and other family members of the victims expressed that although they were deeply hurt and grieving, they forgave the person that murdered their loved ones.[3] This act of forgiveness represents a true example of what it means to surrender hate.

In order to surrender hate, you should first be honest with yourself and admit to yourself that you may have things you strongly dislike and have biases and prejudices against. You should confess that there are things, behaviors, and even people that you have ill feelings toward. Along with admitting we all have things we need to "let go" of, we may need to gain control over some areas of our lives, personalities, and behavioral responses so we can better control our emotions and responses to some of our deep-seated feelings about a person or group of people.

Amid any conflict, one way to minimize your emotions is to simply breathe. Take long, slow, deep breaths while engaging in conversation with the other person. If you find that the situation has escalated beyond a level that you can handle, take some time to cool off and even consider walking away for a short period of time or for as long as you need.

Emotional responses are complex and can be positive or negative. Positive responses include asking for and granting forgiveness, living beyond the negative consequences of out of control and violent responses, and giving another person the gift of your understanding. Negative emotional responses include yelling, screaming, hitting someone, slapping them, and engaging in other forms of physical violence. This could cause bodily harm, injuries, or physical/psychological pain. This could even lead to you and/or the other person being arrested, going to jail, losing your job, and causing trauma and grief. The bottom line is that negatives can be avoided if you focus on the positive and do your best to control your emotions.

Detaching from Negative Emotions

I believe that just as hate is a learned emotion, people can learn *not* to hate. Prayer, praise, and patience with oneself and others will lead to better control of your thoughts, actions, and outcomes.

Learn strategies to manage your anger and seek opportunities to expose yourself to other cultures, customs, and belief systems. Develop an ongoing practice of prayer. All of these actions will help you to manage your emotions.

The first sign of change is recognizing the need to change.

Once a person admits they need to change their belief systems, behaviors, and actions toward another person or group of people, and they make up their minds to do so, they can do so! Decide today to detach from negative emotions.

You can do anything you put your mind and heart to with God's help. It is fine to seek the help of a trusted support system: parents, spouse, family, friends, faith or religious leadership, psychological counselor, healthcare professionals, educators, coaches, positive influencers, etc.

Compromise

In recent years, especially due to the influence of our political administrations, compromise has become somewhat of a dirty word. Compromise is neither dirty nor weak.

Compromise promotes mutual agreement, fair and truthful policies for all people. Positive outcomes from opposing viewpoints can be reached through compromise.

We must learn to seek the greater good for the continuation of our lives and existence as we know it. In the unfortunate situation of divorce, both parties may have to compromise on things like marital assets. In other instances, compromise might dictate one party accepting a less favorable outcome than originally anticipated. If you are involved in a conflict that involves a gun or other dangerous weapons, the opportunity for compromise may not exist. In this instance, your natural survival instincts should kick into gear. Fight or flight is innate. God gave us the internal knowledge to know what to do in an extremely dangerous encounter. If this does happen, engage in compromise but exit, leave, and live to see another day.

Always seek a win-win resolution so that all parties involved benefit. Honesty, truth, and trust are at the heart of every positive negotiation where each party walks away feeling as if their individual needs and wants are met at a satisfactory level. Both parties must be actively engaged and are responsible for the win-win outcome. It may cost you to compromise. You may be required to release your anger and let go of negative emotions. Compromise may not be easy, but it may be necessary to resolve conflict peacefully.

Resolving conflict peacefully is critical if we are to live together in harmony. It is not easy to live peacefully, particularly in a world that glorifies violence in popular music, movies, and on social media. Living peacefully is possible and will require intention.

Review the steps for resolving conflict peacefully with your children. Reflect on a recent conflict that occurred in your life. What did you do to resolve the conflict? Is there anything you could have done differently? Reflect and discuss how you listened, used empathy, surrendered hate, detached from negative emotions, and compromised.

Review the scenario presented below. Help your child outline what he/she could do to bring the conflict to a peaceful end.

Scenario: You are at school and your classmate falsely accuses you of copying her work and stealing her ideas. How can you resolve this? How can you listen, use empathy, surrender hate, detach from negative emotions, and compromise?

Talk with your child and reflect on a real conflict in his/her life presently. Guide him/her through the possible actions to resolve the conflict peacefully. Remember to discuss and offer suggestions on how he/she should listen, use empathy, surrender hate, detach from negative emotions, and compromise.

Peaceful living can be achieved. One of the most important tools in conflict resolution is prayer. I offer this prayer to you. Please pray it with your children. Allow your children to read it aloud to you as well.

Prayer

Thank you Father!
You are the God of creation.
Only you are in control of all things.
Help, strengthen, lead, guide, protect and save me.
Make a way oh Lord.
Send your Holy Spirit to comfort and guide me through any
and every situation I may face.
Make it where both myself and whomever I have conflict
with today go home alive, safely and in peace, freedom and
love.
In the Holy Name of Jesus I ask.

Amen!

Surrender Your Hate
ACTION PLAN

1. Pray every day, all throughout the day!

2. Think positive, good, happy, right thoughts! Positive thinking leads to positive behaviors. Positive behaviors minimize your chances of making bad choices that lead to negative outcomes and possibly death.

3. Take care of your health. Eat right, rest and exercise.

4. Avoid unhealthy activities like drugs, alcohol, illegal actions and violence.

5. Stay away from mean, unkind, selfish, lawless, violent people. These type of people do exist and can often be difficult to discern. Ask a parent, family, teacher, pastor or trusted adult for advice if needed.

Surrender Your Hate
ACTION PLAN

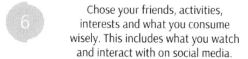

6 Chose your friends, activities, interests and what you consume wisely. This includes what you watch and interact with on social media.

7 Don't hate yourself, or anyone else. Strive to have high self-love and self-esteem.

8 Be kind, gentle, humble, smart, obedient, honest, truthful, and respectful to others and animals.

9 Be aware and cautious while living every day. It's okay to have fun but be safe while doing what you enjoy, e.g. sports, work, hanging out with friends, driving, working out and other activities.

10 Learn, work, share, communicate, manage your tone, emotions, anger, yourself and all situations you find yourself in as best you can.

 LOVE, SURRENDER YOUR HATE, seek righteousness, peace and joy. Help others do the same. **LET LIFE LIVE** - your life and the lives of others, including animals - GOD created them too.

It should not have taken all of this violence, hatred, and evil for me to act on behalf of God's commandments and start this ministry, this movement to encourage, inspire and hopefully influence people – the world – to stop killing its people.

It should not have taken all the deaths from the Covid-19 pandemic and my own near-death experience for me to act on a lifelong urging from God to begin a mission to tell the world to stop killing, maiming, violating, raping, trafficking, and hating!

It should not have taken church and synagogue shootings, bombings, daily street shootings, college campus and elementary school murders, and all other senseless, hateful acts of violence to get me to start encouraging peace and love!

God's plan is one of peace and love, kindness, gentleness, righteousness, joy, and family. The fruits of the spirit!

Unfortunately, it did take some or all of these life-taking, life-ending acts of hate and violence for me to act and to develop a plan to take action to ask all of the world's eight billion people to look within themselves to surrender and eliminate the hatred and evil in our hearts!

World of People: This means all people: young/old, rich/wealthy/poor, man/woman/child, black/white/brown/yellow, and all other nationalities, all faiths, all religions, and/or the lack thereof. Surrender Your Hate! Let life live – today, every day!

Let's work together to save humanity!

To Work Daily: Every day, to live God's plan for his creation. His people!

I ask you: What is it going to take for *you* to join me in this daily action plan to help stop the violence and stop killing ourselves? These are not rhetorical questions! Please ask and answer these questions. And when you do, please share your answer and join me in this mission, this ministry, this hope to surrender our hate and to stop the killing of our God-given lives throughout the entire world.

There is no reason that's good enough for us to continue killing the humanity of this world! Killing each other is not God's plan! His plan is love, not hate! *SURRENDER YOUR HATE – TODAY, EVERY DAY AND LET LIFE LIVE!*

Harden not our hearts toward our fellow human!

Resources

Here are some resources to assist you with your various needs on your path to surrendering hate, turning hate into love, and reducing and preventing violence of any form towards yourself or another human being!

https://www.redcross.org/
American Red Cross

https://blacklivesmatter.com/
Black Lives Matter

https://www.bradyunited.org/
Brady United – Coalition to Stop Gun Violence

https://www.everytown.org/
Everytown for Gun Safety

https://giffords.org/people/coalition-to-stop-gun-violence/
Coalition to Stop Gun Violence

https://frost.house.gov/
Congressman Maxwell Frost

https://www.justice.gov/
Department of Justice

https://www.cdc.gov/violenceprevention/firearms/index.html
Firearm Violence Prevention

https://innocenceproject.org/
Innocence Project

https://iansa.org/
International Action Network on Small Arms

https://www.juvenilejusticeonline.org/en/home
Juvenile Justice Online

https://www.letlifeliveinc.org/
Let Life Live

https://momsdemandaction.org/
Moms Demand Action

https://nationalactionnetwork.net/
National Action Network

https://www.nami.org/Home
National Alliance on Mental Illness

https://naacp.org/
National Association for the Advancement of Colored People

https://www.nabh.org/
National Association for Behavioral Healthcare

https://www.nacrj.org/
National Association of Community and Restorative Justice

https://www.nea.org/nea-today/all-news-articles/do-restorative-practices-work
National Education Association – Restorative Justice Practices

https://www.nih.gov/
National Institutes of Health

https://www.nimh.nih.gov/
National Institute of Mental Health

https://nul.org/
National Urban League

https://www.salvationarmyusa.org/usn/
Salvation Army

https://www.sandyhookpromise.org/
Sandy Hook Promise

https://www.samhsa.gov/find-help/national-helpline
Substance Abuse and Mental Health Services Administration

https://988lifeline.org/
Suicide and Crisis Lifeline

https://surrenderyourhate.com/
Surrender Your Hate

https://www.unodc.org/
United Nations Office on Drugs and Crime

https://www.vera.org/
Vera Institute of Justice

https://vpc.org/
Violence Policy Center

https://www.whitehouse.gov/ogvp/
White House Office of Gun Violence Prevention

About the Author

Michael Bernard Allen is an entrepreneur, business professional, author, human rights consultant, and founder. Michael is the visionary founder of the impactful Surrender Your Hate, LLC., a God-inspired spiritual and social movement. At its core, Surrender Your Hate is on a mission to help people let go of hate, anger, and differences that often lead to violence. Michael is also the founder of Let Life Live, Inc., a 501(c)(3) nonprofit organization whose mission is to take a stand by standing down on (gun) violence. Michael dares to envision a world where the killing of humanity ceases, and his work with Surrender Your Hate and Let Life Live, Inc. is a testament to his commitment to achieving this profound goal.

In 2021, after over three decades of service in the pharmaceutical industry, Michael made a courageous decision to resign from various roles such as Salesperson, Sales Trainer, Manager, Marketer, Sales Director, Diversity Equity and Inclusion Champion, and Senior Sales Operations Leader. This pivotal moment marked the beginning of a new chapter in Michael's life – a chapter dedicated to spreading a powerful message of surrendering hate and fostering unity.

Michael is a 1985 graduate of Florida Agricultural and Mechanical University in Tallahassee, Florida, with a bachelor's degree in journalism and public relations. Michael is a Christian – a worker for Jesus Christ. He is the father of one son, Zachary Christian Allen, a brother to his sisters, Deborah Rimes and Marveen Zanders Jefferson, and the proud son of his mother, Hazel D. Rimes, and father, Ernest L. Allen. This family connection adds a deeply personal dimension to Michael's commitment to creating a world of love, understanding, and compassion.

Notes

1   Liu, S., Xiao, W. S., Xiao, N. G., Quinn, P. C., Zhang, Y., Chen, H., Ge, L., Pascalis, O., & Lee, K. (2015). Development of visual preference for own- versus other-race faces in infancy. *Developmental Psychology, 51*(4), 500–511.

2   Halpern, J. (1993). Empathy: Using resonance emotions in the service of curiosity. *Empathy and the Practice of Medicine*. New Haven, CT: Yale Univ Pr, 160-73.

3   Zook, B. K. B. (2020, October 27). From grief to grace: Overcoming pain with forgiveness. *Essence*. https://www.essence.com/lifestyle/health-wellness/grief-grace-overcoming-pain-forgiveness/

*All scripture quotations are from the Holy Bible, King James Version.

Index

Thank you for buying, reading, and sharing this book published by

POSITIVE PUSH PRESS

Positive Push Press, LLC.

www.PositivePushPress.com

To receive special offers, bonus content, and information about our latest publications, sign up and join our mailing list.

The author, Michael B. Allen, is available for speaking engagements such as keynote speaker, workshop or conference facilitator, session designer, or consultant upon request. Additionally, the author can provide customized consulting services. Please contact Positive Push Press, LLC for additional information at info@PositivePushPress.com or visit the Surrender Your Hate website at https://surrenderyourhate.com/

This book is available at special quantity discounts for bulk purchases. Special excerpts also can be created to fit specific needs. For details, contact info@PositivePushPress.com. For permission to reprint any portion of this book, please contact our permissions department by emailing info@PositivePushPress.com

Stay connected to us: www.PositivePushPress.com

Made in the USA
Columbia, SC
06 December 2024

47458851R00072